DATE DUE

Demco No. 62-0549

Would You Survive?

THE LEARNING RESOURCE CENTER
Weston Intermediate School

Chicago, Illinois

© 2006 Raintree
Published by Raintree,
A division of Reed Elsevier, Inc.
Chicago, Illinois

Customer Service   888–363–4266

Visit our website at www.heinemannraintree.com

Printed and bound in the United States by
Lake Book Manufacturing, Inc.

10 09 08 07 06
10 9 8 7 6 5 4 3 2 1

**Library of Congress Cataloging-in-
Publication Data**
Townsend, John, 1955-
    Would you survive? : living things in habitats /
John Townsend.
        p. cm.
    Includes bibliographical references.
    ISBN 1-4109-1938-2 (library binding) -- ISBN 1-
4109-1969-2 (pbk.)
    1. Adaptation (Biology)--Juvenile literature.   I.
Title.
    QH546.T69 2004
    578.4--dc22
                                    2005009548

Acknowledgments
The author and publishers are grateful to the
following for permission to reproduce copyright
material: Alamy pp. 12–13 (Ace Stock Ltd), 26–27
(Royal Geographical Society), 28 (Ace Stock Ltd);
Corbis pp. 14–15 (Royalty-Free); Getty Images
pp. 8–9 (PhotoDisc), 28–29 (Digital Vision); Lonely
Planet Images pp. 6–7 (Christopher Groenhout);
Nature Picture Library pp. 10–11 (David Curl), 16–17
(David Tipling), 18–19 (Neil Nightingale), 19 top
(Asgeir Helgestad), 22–23 (Leo and Mandy
Dickinson), 29 (David Curl), 29 (Neil Nightingale);
NHPA pp. 17 and 29b (B. & C. Alexander);
Photolibrary.com pp. 20–21 and 29 (Daniel Cox),
24–25 and 29 (John Downer), 29 (Daniel Cox), 29
(John Downer); Science Photo Library p. 22
(BSIP/Platriez); Taxi pp. 4–5 (Getty Images).

Cover photograph of a skull in a desert, reproduced
with permission of Superstock (Age Fotostock).

The publishers would like to thank Nancy Harris and
Harold Pratt for their assistance in the preparation of
this book.

Every effort has been made to contact copyright
holders of any material reproduced in this book.
Any omissions will be rectified in subsequent
printings if notice is given to the publishers.

The paper used to print this book comes from
sustainable resources.

Disclaimer
All the Internet addresses (URLs) given in this book
were valid at the time of going to press. However,
due to the dynamic nature of the Internet, some
addresses may have changed, or sites may have
changed or ceased to exist since publication. While
the author and publishers regret any inconvenience
this may cause readers, no responsibility for any
such changes can be accepted by either the author
or the publishers.

Contents

Some words are printed in bold, **like this**. You can find out what they mean on page 30. You can also look in the box at the bottom of the page where they first appear.

Would You Survive?

Imagine you are lost in a hot desert. You are on your own. There is no water. The sun is beating down. The heat is drying up your mouth. You will die if you don't find water soon. A dust storm starts blowing. It's hard to breathe through the dust.

Our planet isn't ▶ *always friendly to people. Yet other animals can survive where we can't.*

You probably wouldn't survive for long in a hot desert. Yet some animals and plants can survive there. A hot desert may be the home of a rattlesnake, for example.

A **habitat** is the place where a plant or animal normally lives or grows. Animals and plants can survive in many habitats where people cannot. Animals and plants can survive because they have special body parts. These body parts help them live in their surroundings. The special body parts help them to survive.

Basic needs

*All living things need water, food, and air to survive. They all need the right **temperature** to survive. Some animals live in cold places, others in warm. Their habitat gives them these things.*

Surviving in Hot Deserts

Australia has one of the world's largest hot deserts. This desert has a dry **climate**. In general, it gets very little rain and it is very hot. People die there every year. They die from overheating and thirst. People cannot survive for more than a few days without drinking water.

Two explorers tried to cross Australia's desert in 1860. They were named Robert Burke and William Wills. These men were trying to walk across Australia from south to north. However, their food and water ran out. They couldn't go on in the heat without water. They were a long way from help. Both men died near a place called Cooper's Creek. They could not survive in the desert **habitat**.

climate   type of weather usually found in a part of the world

▼ The **temperature** in Australia's hot desert can reach 122 °F (50 °C) during the day.

Deserts

A place is called a desert if very little rain falls there. A desert can be hot or cold. The Sahara Desert, in North Africa, is a hot desert. Antarctica is a cold desert.

Cool camels

The first people to go into Australia's desert brought horses to carry the water. Yet the horses carrying the water needed water, too. The desert was too hot for the horses. So, what else could carry all the water? Camels, of course!

People took camels into the Australian desert over 160 years ago. Many were set free. They lived in the wild. Camels can survive for many days without drinking water. They even feel at home in dust storms! The labels on the picture show you how camels are **equipped** to survive in a hot desert.

A camel closes its nostrils to keep out dust.

A quick drink

When camels find water, they can drink 26 gallons (100 liters) in a few minutes!

A camel has two pairs of eyelids. One pair is clear. A camel can close them during a dust storm and still see.

equipped	have something that is needed
fat	layer under the skin

The hump stores **fat**. The fat is used by the camel when there is no food to eat.

Camels don't lose water by sweating. This means they can survive for days without a drink.

Water-holding frogs

In general, the weather is dry in the Australian desert. It has a dry **climate**. Sometimes it doesn't rain for years. Plants and animals need to be able to store water when this happens. The desert frog has a clever way of surviving when it does not rain for a long time.

Many frogs need to live near water. A desert **habitat** is the last place you would expect to find frogs. Yet Australia's desert is full of them. The desert frog lives in muddy ponds. These ponds dry up if it does not rain for a long time. The frog soaks up the last of the water before this happens. It gets bigger as a special part of its body fills with water.

Then, the frog digs into the ground and waits. Sometimes it has to wait for years. The frog wakes up again when it rains. Being able to store water lets the frog survive in the hot desert.

▼ A desert frog can survive for years without drinking water.

Water-finding roots

Some types of plant can survive in a hot desert. Plants called cacti (one is called a cactus) grow well in a desert **habitat**. They have special parts to help them survive.

There are almost 2,000 types of cactus. Cacti are found in hot deserts such as Arizona. The saguaro cactus is at home here. The labels on the picture show how it copes with so little water.

Giant cacti

Saguaro cacti often live for 200 years. They may grow to a height of 49 feet (15 meters) and weigh up to 11 tons (10 tonnes).

12

root   part of the plant that grows under the soil
stem   main stalk or trunk of a plant

These spikes don't dry up like leaves do. They also stop hungry animals from eating the cactus.

The **stem** of the cactus has a thick skin. This skin stops the inside of the cactus from drying out.

Cactus **roots** spread out near the surface. The roots can then catch rain as soon as it falls.

13

Surviving in Cold Deserts

Antarctica has a dry **climate**. This means it gets very little rain. It is known as a cold desert. There is very little **moisture**, even though the ground is covered in snow.

Parts of Antarctica get less rain than the Australian desert. It can stay frozen all year. Very few living things can survive. The only people that live there are a few scientists. They have to live in heated buildings.

Much of Antarctica is ▶ too cold for most plants or animals to survive.

moisture   small amount of liquid

People have died from the cold in Antarctica. Captain Robert F. Scott hoped to be the first person to reach the South Pole. He and his team set off in 1911. They crossed Antarctica but became stuck in a snowstorm. Scott's frozen body was found eight months later.

The coldest place

Antarctica is the coldest place on Earth. The lowest **temperature** ever recorded was -128.6 °F (-89.2 °C) in July 1983.

Warm birds on ice

Even people wearing thick clothes find it hard to survive in the Antarctic. Yet animals can raise their young there. How can the animals survive the cold?

Penguins are a special type of bird. They cannot fly. They are great swimmers. They are also **equipped** to survive in **habitats** where the **climate** is cold. The emperor penguin raises its young during the winter in Antarctica. The special body parts that help penguins survive are labeled on the photo.

Emperor penguins survive ▶ by huddling together for warmth. They take turns sitting on the outside of the group, where it is coldest.

Thick **fat** keeps the penguin's body heat in.

Feathers trap air around the penguin. This helps to keep the penguin warm.

Feet are also covered by fat and feathers.

Penguin tricks

When penguins are on ice, their blood flows away from their feet. It flows to the rest of their body. This stops the blood from freezing. Humans standing barefoot on ice would quickly get frozen toes.

17

On top of the world

The Arctic is like the Antarctic. It is a cold desert. People find it hard to live there. It is a difficult **habitat** for people to survive in. Very few people live in the Arctic. But plants do!

Lichen is a tiny plant that can survive under a layer of ice. It does not need soil to grow. It can grow on bare rock. Lichen can hold just enough **moisture** (water) to survive. Lichen slowly breaks down the rock it is growing on. Rock dust makes very thin soil. Then, moss and other plants can grow in the thin soil.

Arctic lichens come ▶
in many colors,
even orange.

Moss carpet

Thick moss covers large parts of the Arctic. Moss grows where there is enough soil and moisture. Other plants and animals feed on this moss.

▲ A type of reindeer called caribou feeds on moss.

Thick fur traps warm air all around the body and keeps out the cold.

A thick layer of fat keeps in the body heat.

energy ability to move or do work

Giant of the snow

Another animal that survives in the Arctic is the polar bear. It loves ice and snow. How does a polar bear survive in the cold **climate**?

Polar bears eat seals. The body of a seal has a thick layer of **fat** under the skin. Polar bears build up a layer of fat in their own bodies by eating seals. This layer of fat keeps polar bears warm. It is also a source of **energy** during the winter. Polar bears can live off the layer of fat when no other food can be found.

Long-distance swimmers

Polar bears can swim up to 60 miles (100 kilometers) a day in the icy Arctic water!

Fur keeps the paws warm.

Surviving in High Mountains

People die every year climbing mountains. This is not just because mountains are cold, rocky, and steep. It's the air. Climbers can get sick above 7,900 feet (2,400 meters). There is very little **oxygen** in the air at this height. Air that does not have much oxygen is called "thin" air.

People will die if they don't breathe in enough oxygen. Most climbers take oxygen tanks with them. People cannot stay in high mountains for long. Yet some animals and plants grow strong and healthy there!

◄ *This climber is being given oxygen.*

oxygen   gas in the air that all living things need

◀ Mount Everest is the highest mountain in the world. It is 29,035 feet (8,850 meters) high.

A dangerous climb

Reinhold Messner and Peter Habeler climbed Mount Everest without taking oxygen with them. It was very dangerous. They needed special training.

At home in the clouds

Surviving at a great height isn't a problem for some living things. Some types of geese can fly very high. Bar-headed geese fly at 29,500 feet (9,000 meters). They fly right over Mount Everest! There is very little **oxygen** in the air at this height. The **temperature** is very low. So, how do the geese survive in this high-up world?

The bodies of bar-headed geese are very good at taking in oxygen from the air. They can take in enough to survive even at great heights. The human body cannot take in oxygen well at this height. It would "shut down."

Why don't these birds freeze to death? Bar-headed geese have a layer of **fat** and thick feathers. These special body parts are perfect for keeping out the cold.

High fliers

The highest fliers are Ruppell's griffon vultures. These birds have hit airplanes flying at 39,000 feet (12,000 meters). Luckily, this doesn't happen very often.

Feathers trap air and keep out the cold.

Layers of fat keep the warmth in.

Bodies are very good at taking in oxygen

25

What's Needed for Survival?

No plant or animal (including people) can survive without certain things. Every living thing needs a **habitat**. A habitat has the right amounts of water, food, **oxygen**, and warmth. Plants and animals are **equipped** to survive in habitats where there are different amounts of these four things.

People are able to travel to extreme habitats and learn about them. We can then find ways to survive in such places. People know how to survive in many extreme habitats. Science helps us understand how to stay alive. By using the right equipment, we can control our water, food, air, and **temperature**. People have even survived on the moon by doing this!

BEEF STEW
& DUMPLINGS

▲ *Humans need to stay warm to survive in cold habitats.*

Survival Quiz

Plants and animals are **equipped** to survive in their **habitats**. See if you remember how the living things shown here survive. Answer these three questions for each of the living things from around the world:

1. What is it?

2. Where does it survive?

3. How is it equipped to survive in its habitat?

D

Answers:

A 1) polar bear 2) Arctic (cold desert) 3) **fat** and fur keep it warm in freezing weather

B 1) lichen 2) Arctic (cold desert) 3) needs very little soil and **moisture**

C 1) bar-headed goose 2) very high (above Mount Everest), 3) fat and feathers keep it warm and body needs little **oxygen**

D 1) cactus 2) hot desert (Arizona) 3) water stored in **stem**, thick waxy skin, spikes, and long **roots**

E 1) desert frog 2) hot desert (Australia) 3) fills up with water and burrows underground until rain falls

F 1) emperor penguin 2) Antarctica (cold desert) 3) fat and feathers keep it warm (and they huddle together)

28

Glossary

climate type of weather usually found in a part of the world. The Australian desert has a hot, dry climate.

energy ability to move or do work. Polar bears usually get energy from the food they eat.

equipped having something that is needed. Camels are equipped to survive in hot, dry places.

fat layer under the skin. Fat can help an animal stay warm.

habitat place where a plant or animal normally lives or grows. The habitat of a shark is the sea.

moisture small amount of liquid. A small amount of moisture can be enough for some plants to live on.

oxygen gas in the air that all living things need. Oxygen has no taste, color, or smell.

root part of the plant that grows under the soil. Roots absorb and store water as well as hold plants in place.

stem main stalk or trunk of a plant. A stem often develops buds and shoots and usually grows above the ground.

temperature how hot or cold something is. The temperature in the Australian desert is usually very high during the day.

Want to Know More?

Books

- Parker, Steve. Adaptation. Chicago: Heinemann Library, 2001.
- Royston, Angela. Deserts. Chicago: Raintree, 2004.
- Royston, Angela. Mountains. Chicago: Raintree, 2004.

Websites

- http://www.nwf.org/backyardwildlifehabitat/ Do you want to learn how to create a habitat for animals in your backyard? This cool site will show you how! Sponsored by the National Wildlife Federation.

Find out about the fearsome predators that live in your own garden in *The War in Your Backyard*.

Some animals have amazing athletic skills! Find out which ones in *Super-Flea and Other Animal Champions*.

Index

A Note to Parents and Teachers

Kids can imagine, kids can laugh and kids can learn to read with this exciting new series of first readers. Each book in the Kids Can Read series has been especially written, illustrated and designed for beginning readers. Humorous, easy-to-read stories, appealing characters and topics, and engaging illustrations make for books that kids will want to read over and over again.

To make selecting a book easy for kids, parents and teachers, the Kids Can Read series offers three levels based on different reading abilities:

Level 1: Kids Can Start to Read

Short stories, simple sentences, easy vocabulary, lots of repetition and visual clues for kids just beginning to read.

Level 2: Kids Can Read with Help

Longer stories, varied sentences, increased vocabulary, some repetition and visual clues for kids who have some reading skills, but may need a little help.

Level 3: Kids Can Read Alone

More challenging topics, more complex sentences, advanced vocabulary, language play, minimal repetition and visual clues for kids who are reading by themselves.

With the Kids Can Read series, kids can enter a new and exciting world of reading!